HOW DINOSAURS DEEP?

BEN KITCHIN
ILLUSTRATED BY VICKY FIELDHOUSE

NEW FRONTIER PUBLISHING

Jim was learning how to swim. He had just gone up from the
baby pool to the middle-sized pool.

'Don't worry,' said his mum. 'It's not that deep. I don't think the
middle-sized pool would even come up to a Stegosaurus's knee!'
'Really?' said Jim as he edged away from the water.
'A Stegosaurus must be big! How deep can water get?'

'Deep,' said his mum. 'Some watery places are
deeper than others.'
'How many dinosaurs deep is a fishbowl?' asked Jim.
'One Microceratops standing nice and straight but a
Stegosaurus would hardly wet its toes.'

'How many dinosaurs deep is the bath?'
'Probably a Placodus would have to hold its breath but a
Stegosaurus would just be ankle-deep.'

'What about the big pool? How many dinosaurs
deep is the big pool?'
'Hmmm ... you might just be able to see three Oviraptors
standing on each other's shoulders but a Stegosaurus
would be shoulder-deep.'

'How many dinosaurs deep is the water at the end of the jetty?'
'Our jetty goes deep, so a Stegosaurus with a snorkel or maybe
two Talaruruses playing at acrobatics would be about right.'

'That *is* deep. How many dinosaurs deep is the river at Uncle Barry's shack?'

'Too deep for a Stegosaurus that can't swim! One Tyrannosaurus Rex on its tippy-toes could just manage.'

'What about the blue lake near Nanna's house? How many
dinosaurs deep is that?'
'About five Iguanodons giving each other a boost or one
brilliant Brachiosaurus!'

Jim scratched his head and thought for a while before he finally asked, 'Mum, where is the deepest water in all the world?'

'The great Pacific Ocean! In the Pacific Ocean there is a place so deep and so dark that only the strangest of creatures live down there. It's called the Mariana Trench. Eleven kilometres of water straight down! That's . . . about 687 Brachiosauruses standing on one another's heads or 11 000 little boys deep! So be sure your doggy paddle is working properly before you dive into the water there!'

'You're right, Mum!' said Jim with big wide eyes. 'I don't think I
have anything to worry about in the middle-sized pool.
It's just Stegosaurus-knee-deep!'

EVERYTHING YOU NEED TO

STEGOSAURUS
(STEG-oh-SAWR-us)

Stegosaurus was a plant-eating dinosaur with armoured plates running down its back. Meat eaters had to watch out for its spiky tail which it would use to defend itself. Stegosauruses could grow big! Some grew up to 9m long (30 feet) and 2.75m tall (9 feet), and weighed as much as 3100kg (6800 pounds). But, incredibly, a Stegosaurus's brain was only as big as a walnut!

MICROCERATOPS/MICROCERATUS
(MY-cro-SER-ah-tops/MY-cro-SEH-rah-tus)

Microceratops/Microceratus was a very small dinosaur that lived in North America and Asia around 70 million years ago. It used its parrot-like beak to munch up ferns and other plants. Microceratops/Microceratus was tiny by dinosaur standards, only 30cm tall (1 foot), 80cm long (2.6 feet) and 10kg (22 pounds) in weight. Paleontologists think it was a fast and agile dinosaur, which it would have needed to be to escape some of the bigger meat eaters!

PLACODUS
(PLACK-oh-dus)

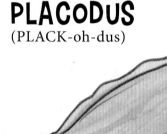

Placodus was a marine reptile that swam in shallow seas around 240 million years ago. It ate shellfish and crustaceans. Paleontologists have studied Placodus skeletons and they believe the big lizards weren't great swimmers or runners as they had heavy rib bones and rigid spines. Adult Placoduses grew up to 40cm tall (1.3 feet) and 2m long (6.5 feet), and could weigh as much as 90kg (200 pounds).

OVIRAPTOR
(oh-vee-RAP-tor)

The name Oviraptor is Latin for 'egg thief'. The first Oviraptor skeleton ever discovered was found beside a nest of eggs so paleontologists thought it might have been trying to pinch them when it died. Now they think the eggs were actually its own but it's been stuck with the name ever since! Oviraptors were bird-like dinosaurs that ran on two legs and grew to about 1m tall (3.3 feet) and 2m long (6.5 feet), and weighed approximately 25–35kg (55–76 pounds).

KNOW ABOUT DINOSAURS

BRACHIOSAURUS
(BRAK-ee-oh-SAW-rus)

Brachiosaurus was one of the tallest and heaviest dinosaurs to ever live. A gigantic plant eater, it could munch on the tops of the tallest trees! Brachiosauruses grew to about 16m tall (52 feet) and 25m long (82 feet), and weighed up to 80 tonnes (176 369 pounds). They had big nostrils on the tops of their heads which gave them a good sense of smell. Too big to be hunted by any of the carnivores of the time, they roamed North America around 144 million years ago.

TYRANNOSAURUS REX
(tie-RAN-o-SAWR-us-rex)

Tyrannosaurus Rex was one of the largest meat eaters to ever walk the planet! Up to 5m tall (16 feet) and 12m long (40 feet), and weighing in at a scary 8 tonnes (17 637 pounds), this is one dinosaur you probably wouldn't want to meet! T-Rexes had short arms and long legs and a huge, tooth-filled head balanced by a long tail.

TALARURUS
(TAH-la-ROO-russ)

Talarurus was a heavily armoured, plant-eating dinosaur about the size of a hippopotamus. Bony spikes and plates all over its body (even on its cheeks) protected it from predators and its clubbed tail could deliver a real wallop! Talaruruses lived in Mongolia 90–95 million years ago and grew up to 1.5m tall (5 feet) and 6m long (20 feet), and weighed as much as 2 tonnes (4480 pounds).

IGUANODON
(ig-WAN-oh-DON)

Iguanodons were plant-eating dinosaurs that could walk on two or four legs. They had toothless beaks and large thumb-spikes which paleontologists believe could have been used to defend themselves or to help them find food. Iguanodons often grew to about 3m tall (10 feet) and 10m long (33 feet), and weighed about 5 tonnes (11 000 pounds).